00147450
979-0-051-66332-3

HAL LEONARD CONCERT BAND SERIES

Gee, Officer Krupke

From

WEST SIDE STORY®

Music by
Leonard Bernstein®

Lyrics by
Stephen Sondheim

Arranged by
Paul Murtha

T0061421

INSTRUMENTATION

1 - Conductor	3 - B♭ Trumpet 1
1 - Piccolo	3 - B♭ Trumpet 2
4 - Flute 1	3 - B♭ Trumpet 3
4 - Flute 2	1 - F Horn 1
2 - Oboe	1 - F Horn 2
2 - Bassoon	1 - F Horn 3
4 - B♭ Clarinet 1	1 - F Horn 4
4 - B♭ Clarinet 2	2 - Trombone 1
4 - B♭ Clarinet 3	2 - Trombone 2
1 - E♭ Alto Clarinet	2 - Trombone 3
2 - B♭ Bass Clarinet	2 - Baritone B.C.
2 - E♭ Alto Saxophone 1	2 - Baritone T.C.
2 - E♭ Alto Saxophone 2	4 - Tuba
2 - B♭ Tenor Saxophone	1 - String Bass
1 - E♭ Baritone Saxophone	2 - Percussion 1
	Drum Set
	4 - Percussion 2
	Police Siren, Cr. Cym., Ratchet,
	Slide Whistle, Wood Block, Tam-Tam
	2 - Mallet Percussion
	Xylophone, Bells
	1 - Timpani

Score (00147450)

LEONARD
BERNSTEIN
Music Publishing
Company LLC

BOOSEY & HAWKES

ISBN-13: 978-1-4950-2692-8

Distributed By
HAL LEONARD

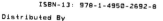

HAL•LEONARD®
CORPORATION
7777 W. BLUEMOUND RD. P.O. BOX 13819 MILWAUKEE, WI 53213

00147450

From WEST SIDE STORY®

GEE, OFFICER KRUPKE

Music by LEONARD BERNSTEIN®
Lyrics by STEPHEN SONDHEIM
Arranged by PAUL MURTHA

Duration – ca. 2:00

Fast, vaudeville style (♩ = 144)

00147450
Gee, Officer Krupke - 2

979-0-051-66332-3

979-0-051-66332-3

979-0-051-66332-3